MW01110483

ISAIAH

Chapters 1–39 by Clifford M. Yeary
Chapters 40–66 by Catherine Upchurch

A ministry of the Diocese of Little Rock
in partnership with Liturgical Press

Dear Friends in Christ,

Sacred Scripture is a wealth of inspired wisdom express-
ing Christian truths which challenge us to deepen our
relationship with God. Although the Bible can be intimi-
dating, it is important that we study God's word in the
Scriptures, because it is the basis of our faith and offers us
the thoughts and experiences of Christians past and
present. It is God speaking to us through the insights of
Church fathers and later saints.

I am pleased to present this study guide from Little Rock
Scripture Study to serve as an aid for reflection and con-
templation in your reading of Scripture. At the same time,
the guide will give you insight into how to apply what you
have read to your life today.

I encourage you to read Sacred Scripture slowly and
reflectively so that it can penetrate your heart and mind.
It is my hope that the Word of God will empower you as
Christians to live a life worthy of your call as a child of God
and a member of the body of Christ.

Sincerely in Christ,

✠ Anthony B. Taylor
Bishop of Little Rock

Sacred Scripture

"The Church has always venerated the divine Scriptures just as she venerates the body of the Lord, since from the table of both the word of God and of the body of Christ she unceasingly receives and offers to the faithful the bread of life, especially in the sacred liturgy. She has always regarded the Scriptures together with sacred tradition as the supreme rule of faith, and will ever do so. For, inspired by God and committed once and for all to writing, they impart the word of God Himself without change, and make the voice of the Holy Spirit resound in the words of the prophets and apostles. Therefore, like the Christian religion itself, all the preaching of the Church must be nourished and ruled by sacred Scripture. For in the sacred books, the Father who is in heaven meets His children with great love and speaks with them; and the force and power in the word of God is so great that it remains the support and energy of the Church, the strength of faith for her sons, the food of the soul, the pure and perennial source of spiritual life."

Vatican II, Dogmatic Constitution on Divine Revelation, no. 21.

INTERPRETATION OF SACRED SCRIPTURE

"Since God speaks in sacred Scripture through men in human fashion, the interpreter of sacred Scripture, in order to see clearly what God wanted to communicate to us, should carefully investigate what meaning the sacred writers really intended, and what God wanted to manifest by means of their words.

"Those who search out the intention of the sacred writers must, among other things, have regard for 'literary forms.' For truth is proposed and expressed in a variety of ways, depending on whether a text is history of one kind or another, or whether its form is that of prophecy, poetry, or some other type of speech. The interpreter must investigate what meaning the sacred writer intended to express and actually expressed in particular circumstances as he used contemporary literary forms in accordance with the situation of his own time and culture.

For the correct understanding of what the sacred author wanted to assert, due attention must be paid to the customary and characteristic styles of perceiving, speaking, and narrating which prevailed at the time of the sacred writer, and to the customs men normally followed in that period in their everyday dealings with one another."

Vatican II, Dogmatic Constitution on Divine Revelation, no. 12.

Instructions

MATERIALS FOR THE STUDY

This Study Guide: Isaiah

Commentary: The New Collegeville Bible Commentary, Old Testament, Volume 13, *Isaiah*, by Leslie J. Hoppe (Liturgical Press), is used with this study. The abbreviation for this commentary, NCBC-OT VOLUME 13, and the assigned pages are found at the beginning of each lesson.

Bible: We highly recommend the *Little Rock Catholic Study Bible* (Liturgical Press), although any version of the New American Bible, Revised Edition (NABRE), or the New Jerusalem Bible will suffice. Paraphrased editions are discouraged as they offer little, if any, help when facing difficult textual questions. Choose a Bible you feel free to write in or underline.

WEEKLY LESSONS

Lesson 1—Isaiah 1–4
Lesson 2—Isaiah 5–11
Lesson 3—Isaiah 12–19
Lesson 4—Isaiah 20–27
Lesson 5—Isaiah 28–32
Lesson 6—Isaiah 33–39
Lesson 7—Isaiah 40–43:8
Lesson 8—Isaiah 43:9–46
Lesson 9—Isaiah 47–50

YOUR DAILY PERSONAL STUDY

The first step is prayer. Open your heart and mind to God. Reading Scripture is an opportunity to listen to God who loves you. Pray that the same Holy Spirit who guided the formation of Scripture will inspire you to correctly understand what you read and empower you to make what you read a part of your life.

The next step is commitment. Daily spiritual food is as necessary as food for the body. This study is divided into daily units. Schedule a regular time and place for your study, as free from distractions as possible. Allow about twenty minutes a day. Make it a daily appointment with God.

As you begin each lesson read the indicated pages of the commentary and the appropriate Scripture passages where indicated. This preparation will give you an overview of the entire lesson and help you to appreciate the context of individual passages.

As you reflect on Scripture, ask yourself these four questions:

1. *What does the Scripture passage say?*
    Read the passage slowly and reflectively. Use your imagination to picture the scene or enter into it.

2. *What does the Scripture passage mean?*
    Read the footnotes and the commentary to help you understand what the sacred writers intended and what God wanted to communicate by means of their words.

3. *What does the Scripture passage mean to me?*
    Meditate on the passage. God's Word is living and powerful. What is God saying to you today? How does the Scripture passage apply to your life today?

4. *What am I going to do about it?*
    Try to discover how God may be challenging you in this passage. An encounter with God contains a challenge to know God's will and follow it more closely in daily life.

THE QUESTIONS ASSIGNED FOR EACH DAY

Read the questions and references for each day. The questions are designed to help you listen to God's Word and to prepare you for the weekly small-group discussion.

Some of the questions can be answered briefly and objectively by referring to the Bible references and the commentary (*What does the passage say?*). Some will lead you to a better understanding of how the Scriptures apply to the church, sacraments, and society (*What does the passage mean?*). Some questions will invite you to consider how God's Word challenges or supports you in your relationships with God and others (*What does the passage mean to me?*). Finally, the questions will lead you to examine your actions in light of Scripture (*What am I going to do about it?*).

Write your responses in this study guide or in a notebook to help you clarify and organize your thoughts and feelings.

THE WEEKLY SMALL-GROUP MEETING

The weekly small-group sharing is the heart of the Little Rock Scripture Study Program. Participants gather in small groups to share the results of praying, reading, and reflecting on Scripture and on the assigned questions. The goal of the discussion is for group members to be strengthened and nourished individually and as a community through sharing how God's Word speaks to them and affects their daily lives. The daily study questions will guide the discussion; it is not necessary to discuss all the questions.

All members share the responsibility of creating an atmosphere of loving support and trust in the group by respecting the opinions and experiences of others, and by affirming and encouraging one another. The simple shared prayer that begins and ends each small group meeting also helps create the open and trusting environment in which group members can share their faith deeply and grow in the study of God's Word.

A distinctive feature of this program is its emphasis on and trust in God's presence working in and through each member. Sharing responses to God's presence in the Word and in others can bring about remarkable growth and transformation.

THE WRAP-UP LECTURE

The lecture is designed to develop and clarify the themes of each lesson. It is not intended to be the focus of the group's discussion. For this reason, the lecture always occurs *after* the small group discussion. If several small groups meet at one time, the groups may gather in a central location to listen to the lecture.

Lectures may be presented by a local speaker. They are also available in audio form on CD, and in visual form on DVD.

Isaiah 1–4

NCBC-OT VOLUME 13, PAGES 5–21

Day 1

Note: Questions 2–5 of this lesson refer to the introduction in the commentary (pp. 5–9).

1. What motivates you to undertake a study of Isaiah?

2. a) Who does the commentary say are the principal characters of the book of Isaiah?

   b) Who are some other important personalities encountered in Isaiah?

3. Why did the early theologians of the church refer to Isaiah as "the fifth gospel"?

Day 2

4. What are the major chapter divisions of Isaiah and what is the importance of these divisions?

5. What does the commentary say is the clear purpose of the book of Isaiah?

6. In what sense are the words of the prophet Isaiah a "vision" (1:1)? (See Mic 1:1.)

Day 3

7. a) When did the kings named during Isaiah's lifetime rule Judah (1:1)?

   b) What were the political and social circumstances of those times?

8. What do the prophet's opening words concerning Israel's betrayal tell us about the nature of God's relationship with Israel (1:2)? (See 49:15; 64:7; Jer 31:9; Hos 11:1.)

9. Why is God rejecting Judah's temple worship (1:10-17)? (See Jer 7:4-5; Hos 6:4-6; Matt 9:13.)

Day 4

10. When have you experienced God's invitation to forgiveness (1:18)? (See Ps 51:9.)

11. What conditions in Judah's society are bringing it into God's judgment (1:22-25)? (See Deut 16:19-20.)

12. a) What will the nations and peoples of the earth go to Jerusalem to find (2:2-3)?

    b) What will be the response of those nations that find what they seek in Jerusalem (2:4)?

Day 5

13. While Isaiah 2:12-17 strongly emphasizes God's judgment, what do these verses have in common with Mary's song (the *Magnificat*) in Luke 1:46-55?

14. What signs of social chaos found in 3:1-9 also afflict, to some degree, societies today? (See Mal 3:23-24.)

15. What role can "healing" play in modern political leadership (3:7)?

Day 6

16. How have you noticed that goodness is its own reward and/or evil acts become their own punishment (3:10-11)? (See Matt 26:52.)

17. A major shift in focus occurs between 4:1 and 4:2. What does this say about God's ultimate intentions for God's people?

18. What memories would Isaiah's promise of "[a] smoking cloud by day and a light of flaming fire by night" (4:5) stir up in the people of Judah? (See Exod 13:21.)

Isaiah 5–11

NCBC-OT VOLUME 13, PAGES 21–43

Day 1

1. From last week's lesson, what do you recall concerning the nature of the prophecies proclaimed by Isaiah?

2. Compare "the song of the vineyard" in Isaiah (5:1-7) with Jesus' parable of the vineyard (Matt 21:33-41). What similarities strike you? What differences stand out to you? (See Jer 2:21; Ezek 19:10-12; Hos 10:1; Luke 13:6-9.)

3. What evil is actually committed by "Those who join house to house, who connect field with field, Until no space remains" (5:8)?

Day 2

4. Describe when you have felt the majestic presence of God, or some other experience of God's presence (6:1-7).

5. What are the seraphim that are part of Isaiah's vision of God in the temple (6:2)? (See Num 21:4-9.)

6. What has God called Isaiah to do (6:8-13)? (See Matt 13:13-17; Acts 28:23-28.)

Day 3

7. Why has King Ahaz of Judah's heart begun to tremble "as the trees of the forest" (7:1-2)? (See 2 Kgs 16:5-7.)

8. a) What sign does Isaiah say God is giving Ahaz to assure him that Judah will survive an attack by Samaria and Aram (7:10-16)?

   b) How is this sign given special importance in the Gospel of Matthew (Matt 1:18-23)?

9. In this section there are three children who are given unusual names. What meanings lie behind the names "Emmanuel" (7:14; 8:8, 10), "Shear-jashub" (7:3), and "Maher-shalal-hash-baz" (8:1-4)?

Day 4

10. a) Instead of military foes, who is the real "rock for stumbling" and "trap" and "snare" that the people of Judah should be fearing (8:12-15)?

    b) How does Paul make use of 8:14 in Romans 9:30-32?

11. What is the promised "great light" that will be given to "those who lived in a land of gloom" (9:1-6)? (See Matt 4:12-17.)

12. When has a child brought great hopes for the future into your life (9:5)?

Day 5

13. What four reasons does Isaiah give for God's pending judgment of the northern kingdom of Israel (9:7-11, 12-16, 17-20; 10:1-4)?

14. It is God who is using Assyria's military might in order to punish Israel (10:5-6). Why, then, does God promise to punish Assyria for its assaults on Israel (10:12-16)?

15. What life lessons have you learned after enduring difficult times (10:20)?

Day 6

16. Who is Jesse and why is he said to be a "stump" (11:1)? (See 1 Sam 16:1-13.)

17. Of the many spiritual gifts to be bestowed on the future king, which would you most fervently pray for in your own life (11:2)?

18. What characteristics would you hope to find in today's religious leaders and elected officials (11:1-5)?

Isaiah 12–19

NCBC-OT VOLUME 13, PAGES 42–58

Day 1

1. Identify a particular passage (perhaps one verse or even several verses) from the previous lesson (Isa 5–11) that stands out in your recollection and briefly explain why it does so.

2. When had the Israelites previously sung a similar song of thanksgiving as that found in 12:1-6? (See Exod 15:1-4.)

3. Which events in your life have been causes for giving God a song of thanksgiving (at least in your heart)?

Day 2

4. In the "Oracles against the Foreign Nations," why, according to the commentary, does Babylon stand at the head of the list (13:1-22)?

5. Isaiah speaks of "the day of the LORD" (13:6). How do other prophets understand the phrase "the day of the LORD" (Joel 2:1-2; Amos 5:18-20; Zeph 1:7-8)?

6. Isaiah 14 predicts rejoicing will come with the end of Babylon's oppression. What historical events are you aware of that have brought great rejoicing to people?

Day 3

7. Who does the commentary identify as the one fallen from heaven (14:12) and how did this figure come to be identified with Satan in Christian history? (See Luke 10:18.)

8. a) What mourning rituals are identified in Isaiah 15:2-3?

   b) What mourning rituals are commonly observed within your local faith community?

9. According to the commentary, what purpose would lead the mourners in Moab to weep in the "high places" (15:2)?

.

Day 4

10. Where does Isaiah predict the outcasts of Moab will go (16:4-5) and what will bring them mercy?

11. What are the historical circumstances that are behind Isaiah linking the fate of Damascus (Aram) with that of Ephraim (the northern kingdom of Israel) in 17:3 (7:1–8:4)? (See 2 Kgs 16:5.)

12. Why will the cities of the northern kingdom be abandoned (17:4, 9-10)? (See Jer 2:32.)

Day 5

13. With what images does Isaiah compare the power of mighty nations with the power of Israel's God (17:12-14)?

14. According to the commentary, what connection is there between Isaiah 17:12-13 and Jesus' calming of the storm in Matthew 8:23-27?

15. Even in the midst of oracles of doom, Isaiah speaks of the nations turning to the Lord (18:7). Do you believe that conversion is possible even for the most wicked? (See Jer 18:7-8.)

Day 6

16. Isaiah's prophecies against Egypt link harsh rule with ecological disaster (19:4-8). What examples of poor government and ecological damage are you aware of in the modern world?

17. a) Why was Isaiah's vision of Israel being the linchpin of eventual unity between Egypt and Assyria so lofty (19:23-25)?

    b) What vision of unity among contentious nations would be equally remarkable today?

18. The commentary states that many modern readers find the Oracles against the Foreign Nations (beginning with Isa 13) difficult to read. What have been your feelings as you read them?

Isaiah 20–27

NCBC-OT VOLUME 13, PAGES 57–72

Day 1

1. What stands out most in your mind as you recall last week's lesson?

2. Why was Egypt trying to form an alliance with Judah during the reign of Sargon II of Assyria (20:1-6)? (See 30:2-5.)

3. a) What "dramatic gesture" did Isaiah perform for three years before the people of Judah and what purpose did it serve (20:1-2)?

   b) How have other prophets used dramatic gesture to communicate God's message? (See Jer 32:1-44; Ezek 4:1-6; Hos 1:1-9.)

Day 2

4. What other great empire of later history does the book of Revelation refer to as Babylon and also proclaim, "Fallen, fallen is Babylon" (Isa 21:9)? (See Rev 14:8; 18:2.)

5. Isaiah 21:13-17 is an oracle against "Kedar." Where was Kedar and what message would this oracle convey to the people of Judah?

6. Why was it wrong for Jerusalem to rejoice at having avoided being attacked by Assyrian forces (22:1-14)?

Day 3

7. In what context does Paul quote Isaiah 22:13 (1 Cor 15:32)? (See Wis 2:1-6.)

8. Who were Shebna and Eliakim (22:15-25)?

9. How does the use of Isaiah 22:22 in Revelation 3:7 transform its meaning?

Day 4

10. a) Where were Tarshish, Tyre, and Sidon located and what was their relationship to each other (23:1-14)? (See Ezek 27:1-8, 12; Jonah 1:3.)

    b) What link to these prophecies against Tyre and Sidon (23:1-17) is found in the gospels (Matt 11:21-22; Luke 10:13-14)?

11. What city is the prophecy in 24:10-13 levied against?

12. Isaiah 24–27 is called the "Apocalypse of Isaiah." What traits does it share with the apocalyptic literature found in Daniel 7–12 and the book of Revelation? (See commentary, p. 66.)

Day 5

13. What works of mercy and justice have you witnessed for which you might give thanks to God as Isaiah does in 25:1-5?

14. a) Why would feasting (25:6) be such a potent symbol of God's renewed rule over the earth?

    b) What banquets do you remember as special encounters with God's love and care for you and your loved ones?

15. How important is the promise in 25:7-9 to your own faith life? (See 1 Cor 15:26, 54-55; 2 Tim 1:10.)

Day 6

16. To what do we owe our ability to worship God (26:3)? (See Gen 1:26-27; Rom 8:15.)

17. a) How does the image of going behind closed doors and hiding from the wrath (26:20-21) recall the Passover of Exodus 12:21-23?

    b) Why would recalling Exodus be of great importance while Israel is being harshly punished?

18. On what positive note does this section of Isaiah close (27:13)?

ch 25 - listen again

praise hope and deliverance
promise of Jesus - prophecy

ch 26 -
Judah

judgment of the Lord

Isaiah 28–32

NCBC-OT VOLUME 13, PAGES 73–88

Day 1

1. What message or insight from the previous lesson stands out most clearly to you?

2. a) Isaiah describes Samaria (capital of Ephraim, or the northern kingdom of Israel) as a once magnificent garland (28:1). To what would you compare your city, town, or countryside?

   b) What strengths and ills do you find in your locality?

3. Why have the priests and prophets of Northern Israel (Ephraim) been unable to teach or speak a message from God (28:7-10)?

Day 2

4. What new meaning does Paul give to Isaiah 28:11-12 (1 Cor 14:21-22)? (See Deut 28:49.)

5. What does the church today warn are signs of a culture that makes a covenant with death?

6. How might one guard against the spiritual danger Isaiah associated with Israel's formal, ritual worship (29:13-14)? (See Mark 7:6-7.)

Day 3

7. When do you feel especially drawn to acknowledge God as your maker (29:15-16)? (See Ps 139:13-14.)

8. Who are the ones who will rejoice to experience what God will do "in a very little while" (29:17-24)?

9. How can one be reliant upon God for all one's needs and still receive "strength" and "protection" in people, places, or things (30:1-2)? (See Matt 6:24-34.)

Day 4

10. What importance does "Rahab" have in the cultural world of Isaiah's time (30:7)? (Job 9:13; 26:12; Ps 89:11.)

11. List the signs that the Lord has become gracious and shown mercy to his people (30:18-26).

12. If you have a New American Bible, Revised Edition (© 2010), what does the footnote to 30:33 explain about the meaning of the "tophet" God has prepared for Assyria?

Day 5

13. What animal symbols does Isaiah use for God in 31:4-5 and how do these symbols help to describe God's care for Jerusalem?

14. How might the events of 2 Kings 19:32-37 relate to Isaiah's prophecy in 31:8-9?

15. What does it mean for rulers and political leaders to be called to be a "shelter from the wind, a refuge from the rain" (32:1-2)?

Day 6

16. What evils are called "Godless" and deceitful in 32:6-7?

17. Identify any spiritual dangers you see today in being complacent due to material well-being (32:9-14). (See Matt 6:19-20; Luke 12:15-21.)

18. What will happen when "the spirit from on high" is poured out (32:15-20)? (See Joel 3:1-5; Acts 2:15-21.)

Isaiah 33–39

NCBC-OT VOLUME 13, PAGES 88–103

Day 1

1. What is something you recall from the previous lesson concerning Isaiah's prophecies of Jerusalem's judgment or eventual salvation?

2. a) Concerning Israel/Judah, what does Isaiah identify as "[t]hat which makes her seasons certain" (33:6)?

   b) In what ways has current uncertainty about seasons (including climate change and weather extremes) become a theological concern among Christians and other people of faith?

3. While the "sinners" in Zion are to be in dread of God's judgment (33:14), what characterizes those who are promised blessing instead (33:15-16)?

Day 2

4. Why might the promise made to Jerusalem in 33:21 be an outlandish one?

5. a) What is the "ban" that Isaiah says God has placed on the nations (34:2)? (See Deut 13:13-19; Josh 6:15-21.)

   b) What do you think Jesus would teach about the "ban"? (See Matt 5:38-48.)

6. What verses indicate that Isaiah 34 is concerned not just with corrupt nations but also with evil on a cosmic level?

Day 3

7. If your Bible has footnotes, what or who does it say is the "lilith" of Isaiah 34:14?

8. What strong contrast with 34:9-17 is depicted in 35:1-10?

9. How are the promises of 35:4-6a used in Matthew 11:2-6?

Day 4

10. Why do Hezekiah's representatives (Eliakim, Shebna, and Joah) ask Sennacherib's commander (Rabshakeh in some translations) to speak to them in Aramaic (36:11)?

11. What are the four major points of the Assyrian commander's message (36:4-10, 12-20)?

12. a) What big difference is there between Isaiah's account of Sennacherib's incursion of Judah (36:1–37:9a) and the nearly identical account in 2 Kings 18:13–20:19?

    b) What might be the reason that Isaiah's account (37:6-7) omitted this information? (See commentary, p. 97.)

Day 5

13. When have you prayed for deliverance from a looming or existing circumstance?

14. a) How did Sennacherib's letter to Hezekiah blaspheme the Lord (37:10-13)?

    b) How does Isaiah's prophecy in 37:22-35 answer Sennacherib's claim to invincibility? (See John 19:10-11.)

15. a) When has God answered a heartfelt prayer of yours (38:1-8)?

    b) How have you given thanks to God for answering prayers? Consider praying Isaiah 38:15-20; Psalm 30; or Psalm 40:1-11.

Day 6

16. Hezekiah praises God, saying, "Parents declare to their children, O God, your faithfulness" (38:19b). When has a parent or elder's witness to God's faithfulness been of significance to your own faith life?

17. a) Why has Hezekiah shown the Babylonian envoys his treasure (39:1-2)? (See 2 Kgs 18:14-16.)

    b) How did Isaiah respond to Hezekiah when he learned what Hezekiah had shown the Babylonians (39:1-7)?

18. Why did Hezekiah express satisfaction at Isaiah's dire prophecy concerning his descendants' fate (39:8)?

Isaiah 40–43:8

NCBC-OT VOLUME 13, PAGES 103–116

Day 1

1. Review the information about the likely time period in which Isaiah 40–55 was produced (pages 6–7 of the introduction to your commentary, as well as the introduction or other notes in your Bible). Why would an awareness of the historical circumstances of this section make a difference in understanding the text?

2. In your own words, summarize how Isaiah 40–55 differs from Lamentations and Deuteronomistic history and other biblical writings about the period of exile. (See commentary, pp. 103–104.)

3. How do the words of Isaiah 40:2 provide the comfort that is spoken of in 40:1? (See 49:13.)

Day 2

4. a) What image from Israel's history is evoked by referencing the way of the Lord in the wilderness (40:3-4)? (See Exod 13:21-22; 40:38; Deut 2:7.)

   b) The passage from Isaiah 40:3 is later used by the gospel writers to speak of the ministry of John the Baptist. How is the passage adapted to help make this application? (See Matt 3:3; Mark 1:2-3; Luke 3:2-6; John 1:23.)

5. When have you experienced the lasting power of God's word in Scripture (40:6)? Perhaps offer an example of how God's word from an ancient time has been effective or meaningful in your life today.

6. Jerusalem is not simply rescued for its own sake but is given a commission (40:9-11) for the sake of all of Judah. What does this tell you about the nature of God's work in our individual and communal lives?

Day 3

7. How does the prophet demonstrate that God is both powerful and gentle in regard to the people in exile (40:10-11)?

8. Describe a time when creation itself convinced you of God's ultimate power in your life or throughout the world (40:12-17). (See Job 38:4ff.; Rom 1:20.)

9. Pray with 40:25-31. Which verse or verses speak most effectively to your life at this time?

Day 4

10. a) Who is the "champion of justice" referenced in 41:2, and what can you learn about him? (See 44:28–45:1; 2 Chr 36:23-24; Ezra 1:2-4.)

    b) Has there ever been a time when you felt God used someone unexpected, or someone outside of our faith tradition, to teach a valuable lesson or do God's work?

11. God's message through the prophet is "Do not fear: I am with you" (41:10, 13). What verbs are used in this section (41:10-20) to demonstrate the ways that God is with Israel/Judah?

12. God's people in exile may have wondered if Babylon's gods were more powerful than their own God. The trial scene of 41:21-29 concludes with God's response through the prophet: "Ah, all of them are nothing, their works are nought, their idols, empty wind!" When have you discovered that some passing devotion or superstition is indeed without the power that you once imagined?

Day 5

13. a) At the time that Isaiah spoke the words we find in 42:1-4, who might he have been referring to?

   b) Why are these verses (42:1-4) and the others that are referred to as "Servant Songs" (49:1-6; 50:4-11; 52:13–53:12) appropriately applied to Jesus in New Testament times?

14. Isaiah 42:6-7 offers a powerful summary of the role of God's covenant people. We, too, are God's covenant people (see Eph 2:13-20; 3:4-6). In what ways do these verses reflect or challenge the role of the church in our day and age?

15. Which of the metaphors or images of God found in the hymn of 42:10-17 is most appealing to you as you stretch your understanding of God, a warrior or a woman in labor?

Day 6

16. The words of the prophet describe the indifference (42:19-20) and stubbornness (42:24) of God's people, failures that brought about their situation of exile. Are there particular passages from the first section of Isaiah (chaps. 1–39) that illustrate their refusal to heed God's warnings and repent?

17. What is the meaning of "ransom" in 43:3? (See Deut 4:37-40.)

18. Isaiah 43:1-9 shifts to a message of hope and redemption, reminding Jacob/Israel that they belong to God. Which of these verses would you like to commit to memory as a reminder of your own value to God?

Isaiah 43:9–46

NCBC-OT VOLUME 13, PAGES 116–127

Day 1

1. What lesson from last week's lecture or group discussion was most helpful to you, and why?

2. What is the gist of the trial scene in 43:9-15? Who is on trial and what proof is given for the defense?

3. a) How does the prophet use the exodus event as a kind of template for God's new action on behalf of Israel (43:16-21)?

   b) And how is this same exodus pattern employed in the New Testament? (See examples in Luke 9:28-31; John 3:14-15; 6:32-35; Col 1:13-14.)

Day 2

4. In a series of contrasts, "you did not" (43:22, 23, 24) vs. "I remember" and "I will" (43:25; 44:3), God offers forgiveness and a renewal of covenant blessings. What does this portrait of God's action on behalf of Israel teach you about forgiveness? (See 1:18; 44:22; Ps 32:1-2; 51:1-14.)

5. In your experience, how has God offered you comfort and assurance when you felt you were unlovable or abandoned (44:2)?

6. Water, especially in a barren landscape, is symbolic of renewal, life, and even prosperity (44:3). (See 35:7; 49:10; Deut 8:15; Ps 65:10.) In what ways is the symbolic power of water continued in Christian practice? (See Acts 8:37-38; Titus 3:4-7.)

Day 3

7. Throughout Scripture God's people are admonished not to fear (44:8). List some of the sources of fear and choose one of these Scripture passages as a reminder that God is with you: 43:1; Joshua 1:9; Matthew 10:28; Luke 1:30; 2 Timothy 1:7; Hebrews 13:6; 1 John 4:18.

8. a) What primary evidence is offered to illustrate that false idols do not have the power that God possesses (44:9, 18-19)? (See 45:16-17; Deut 4:28; Ps 115:4-8.)

   b) In contrast, how is Israel's God portrayed (44:21)?

9. Babylon's destruction of Jerusalem and the temple was historically and spiritually significant. (See 2 Kgs 24:10-17; Lam 1:1-8.) How do you think the message of 44:26-28 would have sounded to the ears of those about to be released from exile?

Day 4

10. Identify Cyrus (44:28), his political position and significance, and the time period when he lived. (See 46:11; 2 Chr 36:22-23; Ezra 1:1-4.)

11. Why was it significant that God through Isaiah identified Cyrus as "My shepherd" (44:28) and the Lord's "anointed" (45:1)?

12. Review these passages and discuss the way that Israel/Judah would have traditionally understood the role of the shepherd (Gen 29:2-3; 1 Sam 17:34-35; Ezek 34:11-16) and someone anointed by God (Exod 29:1-7; 1 Sam 16:12-13; 1 Kgs 19:15-16; Ps 23:5).

Day 5

13. What is the purpose of God's rebuke in 45:8-13?

14. Verses 15 and 19 of chapter 45 almost seem to contradict each other. Could it be that in exile God seemed hidden, but now will be doing something bold and new? How have you experienced both the hiddenness and boldness of God in your life?

15. In what context does Paul use 45:23-24 in his correspondence? (See Rom 14:11; Phil 2:10-11.)

Day 6

16. Although 46:1-2 predicts that Babylon will suffer the fate of most peoples conquered in battle, what does your commentary indicate actually happened after Persia conquered Babylon?

17. God carries Israel from birth into old age (46:3-4). Pray with the words of these verses to consider how God's care for the church has been constant throughout time.

18. Variations of God's declaration "I am the LORD" are found through-out this portion of the book of Isaiah (see 43:3, 11-12, 15; 44:24; 45:5-6, 18, 22; 46:9.) How does God prove in your life that he is the Lord?

Isaiah 47–50

NCBC-OT VOLUME 13, PAGES 126–137

Day 1

1. In the previous lesson, God used a surprising figure, Cyrus, to fulfill his plan (see also 48:14). Describe a time when you became aware that God does not always work in predictable ways or through predictable people.

2. Isaiah is filled with imagery (language that creates a mental picture). After reading through the description of the fall of Babylon (47:1-15), which of the images used by the prophet to describe their doom seems most compelling to you? Why?

3. Babylon is accused of being "secure" in its wickedness and therefore assumes no one sees its evil (47:10). When have you become aware that false security can lead individuals or groups to play by their own rules, assuming they will never be caught? (See Ps 36:2-5.)

Day 2

4. Much like the taunting of the Babylonian Empire in Isaiah 47, the book of Revelation taunts the Roman Empire (Rev 17–18). How do both of these places, once deflated of power, end up serving God's people? (See commentary, p. 128.)

5. What is being referenced in 48:1-2? (See 1:11-13, 16-17; 3:8; Hos 4:1-3.)

6. In what ways has the church been refined and tested "in the furnace of affliction" (48:10)? How have such times affected the church?

Day 3

7. Early in the history of God's people, obedience and prosperity were sometimes linked together (see Deut 11:26-28; 28:1-2). In Isaiah 48:18-19, there is a similar formula. How might obedience have been understood differently in these two periods?

8. The exiles are exhorted not simply to flee the Babylonians, but to tell the story "to the ends of the earth" much like earlier generations told the exodus story (48:20-21). What are some of the key moments of redemption that we Christians proclaim to others?

9. How could the words of 49:1-3 be applied to the prophet Isaiah? And to Israel itself? And to Jesus?

Day 4

10. Why do you suppose the image of being a "light to the nations" (49:6) had such power in its original context and in later generations? (See 49:8, 18, 23; Luke 2:25-32; Acts 1:8; 13:47.)

11. How would you describe the tone of God's words to the exiles in 49:8-13?

12. What experiences have you had or observed that might help to explain why God's people still feel forsaken and forgotten (49:14) even when told they will be liberated?

Day 5

13. "I will never forget you. See, upon the palms of my hands I have engraved you" (49:15-16). How can God's ancient promise to Israel assist you in your own spiritual journey at this time in your life?

14. While the imagery in 49:23-26 is perhaps too graphic for some to digest, it describes the reversal of fortunes God has in store. How is a reversal of fortunes used in the Bible to speak of God's unique power? (See 61:1-3; Ps 126; Matt 5:3-11; Luke 1:46-55; 4:16-21; 6:20-26; Jas 1:9-11.)

15. What does Isaiah tell God's people about the purpose of their exile (50:1)?

Day 6

16. The prophet Isaiah receives from God "a word that will waken" those who are weary (50:4). When have you seen the power of God's word give new energy to those who are weary by life circumstances, injustices, or tragedies?

17. What efforts are you willing to make to "hear as disciples do" in your prayer life? (See Ps 95:7; Prov 22:17-19; Mark 4:3-9.)

18. Select one of the accounts of the passion of Christ from the gospels and consider how the "Servant Song" of 50:4-11 can be applied to Christ.

Isaiah 51–55

NCBC-OT VOLUME 13, PAGES 137–148

Day 1

1. What stands out to you from the previous lesson about the response to the prophet's message of liberation?

2. What is the prophet's purpose in recalling Abraham and Sarah (51:1-3) and the flight from Egypt (51:10-11)? (See Gen 12:1-3; 22:17-18; Exod 14:19-31.)

3. What is the significance of the prophet's repeated references to justice throughout this section (51:1-8)? (See 1:27; 2:2-4; Deut 16:20; 32:4; Ezra 9:15; Ps 37:27-28; 146:5-8.)

Day 2

4. What factors contributed to Israel's need to be awakened (51:17; 52:1)? What factors also make us spiritually drowsy?

5. What is offered as the guarantee that the captives will be released (51:14-16)?

6. a) How does Paul use 52:7 in his letter to the Romans (Rom 10:14-17)?

   b) Who has been an ambassador of the Good News in your life (52:7)?

Day 3

7. When was the last time you were astonished by what you saw God do (53:1)?

8. According to your commentary and biblical footnotes, what are some of the possible meanings of the servant bearing the pain and sufferings of others, being pierced for their iniquities (53:4-6)?

9. In what ways has the church helped to draw out additional understandings of the suffering described throughout the Servant Song (52:13–53:12)? (See Matt 8:16-17; 9:35-36; John 10:11-18; Acts 8:26-35; 1 Pet 2:21-25.)

Day 4

10. The Bible repeatedly highlights the paradox that defeat and death and humiliation never have the final word (53:11-12). (For other examples, see Gen 45:4-8; Esth F:1-9; Jer 31:7-9; healing stories and passion and resurrection stories in the gospels.) What are some ways that we Christians can give witness to this truth?

11. How has the message of redemptive suffering found in the Servant Song (42:1-4; 49:1-6; 50:4-9; 52:13–53:12) affected your attitude toward personal suffering?

12. Who is the "barren one" referred to in 54:1?

Day 5

13. Why would barrenness and its reversal (54:1-3) serve as an appropriate metaphor for the spiritual condition of God's people? (See Gen 18:9-14; 30:22-23; 1 Sam 1:4-11, 20; Ps 113:7-9.)

14. What qualities of the marriage relationship alluded to in 54:4-10 are also the qualities of God's relationship to us?

15. Select a verse in chapter 54 that speaks strongly to you about God's action in your own life and describe why you made your choice.

Day 6

16. How is the promise of abundant water and rich food (55:1-2) fulfilled in Christ? (See Mark 14:22-24; John 4:10-15; 6:26-35; 7:37-39.)

17. By using imperatives ("pay attention," "come to me," "listen," and "seek the LORD," 55:3, 6) Isaiah makes it clear that the returning exiles must actively participate in their liberation. Where might God be using these same imperatives today?

18. Describe some ways in which God's word has proven to be productive and effective in your life in the past year or so (55:10-11).

Isaiah 56–61

NCBC-OT VOLUME 13, PAGES 148–162

Day 1

1. What did you learn in the previous lesson about God's way of giving reassurance that you would like to carry forward with you?

2. Chapter 56 is the beginning of what some believe to reflect a later period in history when the exiles have begun reoccupying Jerusalem. According to 56:1-8, what was required upon returning to Jerusalem to be counted among God's people? (See 58:13-14; Wis 3:14.)

3. How has the wording "a monument and a name" (*yad vashem*, 56:5) been used in modern-day Israel?

Day 2

4. What does your parish do to reinforce the priority of prayer and its openness to all peoples (56:7)?

5. Isaiah shows no tolerance for Israel's unjust and incompetent leaders in this period (56:9–57:13), telling them to rely on their idols when they are in trouble (57:13). How does idolatry still manage to distract us from relying on God? (See Col 3:5.)

6. "I dwell in a high and holy place, but also with the contrite and lowly of spirit" (57:15). How does this verse speak to your experience of God?

Day 3

7. a) What does the prophet describe as true fasting (58:6-10)? (See Zech 7:9-10; Ezek 18:5-9.)

   b) How does this lesson take shape in the New Testament? (See Mark 2:18-20; Matt 25:31-46; Acts 13:2-3; 14:23.)

8. The Middle East is an arid land, largely dependent on irrigation. How would the image of 58:11 have sounded in the ears of those in Jerusalem? What would ensure this kind of reward?

9. a) Why did Sabbath observance become so significant in the years following the exile (58:13-14)?

   b) Describe some ways that we can keep the Sabbath holy, without allowing such observance to become mere ritual (Mark 2:27).

Day 4

10. In 59:1-8, the prophet describes the atmosphere after the return to Jerusalem. Why is it that old rivalries and divisions have emerged so soon after their liberation from Babylon? (See Ezra 4:1-5; Neh 1:1-4.)

11. What is striking to you in the confession of sin found in 59:9-15? And God's response in 59:15-21? (See Neh 1:5-11.)

12. What are the signs that your faith is being passed on to the next generation (59:21)? (See Deut 6:4-9.)

Day 5

13. Isaiah 60:1-6 is proclaimed at Mass on the feast of Epiphany. How does it apply to this feast? (See Ps 72:8-15; Matt 2:1-12.)

14. Chapter 60 elaborately describes former enemies and other nations coming to Jerusalem. What is the apparent message in this context (60:14-16)? (See 61:5-7.)

15. One has only to look at history to see that Israel's people did not realize all the promises described in 60:19-22. How is it possible to experience the truth, "the LORD will be your light forever, your God will be your glory," when the facts seem to work against it? (See Rev 21:22-24.)

Day 6

16. To those who returned from exile and re-established themselves in Jerusalem, what is the message of 61:1-3? And what is the message of these verses in your life when you hear them on the lips of Jesus in Luke 4:18-19?

17. In what sense will Israel be "Priests of the LORD" (61:6)? (See Exod 19:6; Rom 15:15-16.)

18. Justice is the cause of joy for the prophet and all of God's people (61:10-11). What acts of justice have been the cause of joy in your life?

Isaiah 62–66

NCBC-OT VOLUME 13, PAGES 162–173

Day 1

1. In the previous lesson, the scene shifted from Babylon to Jerusalem as Israel returned to rebuild the city and the temple. What has been most surprising to you about this section so far?

2. In Scripture, what is the significance of receiving a new name from God (62:2-4, 12)? (See Gen 17:5, 15-16; 32:25-31; Matt 16:15-18.)

3. Why is the metaphor of marriage often used in Scripture to speak of God's relationship with his people (62:5)? (See 54:5; Hos 2:16-18, 21-22; Eph 5:29-32; Rev 19:7-8.)

Day 2

4. What is the significance of the description of God coming from the direction of Edom as a bloody warrior (63:1-6)? (See 34:5-6; Ezek 25:12-13; Obad 12-14.)

5. In recalling God's deeds on Israel's behalf, the prophet emphasizes that God's very presence is the source of salvation (63:9). When you review your life thus far, in what ways are you more aware of this gift of God's presence?

6. How is the plea to "rend the heavens and come down" (63:19) fulfilled in the Christian tradition? (See Ps 144:5; Mark 1:10; John 1:14; Phil 2:7.)

Day 3

7. Isaiah 64:3-4 offers a good example of the prophet's desire to persuade God to be compassionate in spite of Israel's sin. Are you ever tempted to use persuasive speech in an effort to win God's favor?

8. What does it mean in your spiritual life to "wait for the Lord" (64:3)? (See Ps 27:13-14; 40:2; 69:7; Rom 8:18-19.)

9. Rather than pleading Israel's case as in a courtroom, Isaiah appeals to God as a father and a worker of clay (64:7). How do these images of God change the dynamics of prayer to God? (See 45:9-10; Tob 13:3-4; Wis 15:7; Sir 33:13; Jer 18:1-6; Matt 6:9-15; Rom 8:14-17.)

Day 4

10. What prevented Israel from recognizing God's presence and readiness to act on their behalf (65:1)? What sometimes prevents us from the same awareness?

11. Find out what is significant about Sharon and the Valley of Achor (65:10). (See 35:2; Josh 7:24-26; Hos 2:16-17.)

12. Throughout chapter 65, what phrases or descriptions are used to identify those who respond faithfully to God?

Day 5

13. What is the probable meaning of 65:17 in its original context in Isaiah? And what meaning has it come to have in later times? (See 2 Pet 3:13-14; Rev 21:1-3.)

14. Judaism's inner conflict over the value of worship in the temple vs. the value of living justly (66:1-6) is never fully resolved. How does the same concern surface in the incident surrounding the martyrdom of Stephen in Acts 6:8-15 and 7:39-60?

15. In 66:7-13, Jerusalem and God are both depicted as a mother. How do such images help or challenge your ideas about God? (See 49:15; Ps 131:2; Matt 23:37.)

Day 6

16. In what ways could God's word cause us to tremble in response (66:2, 5)? (See 1 Chr 16:29-30.)

17. Read and pray with 66:18-24, which describes God's vision for the unity of nations around a restored Jerusalem. How can such hope-filled language help to make us a people of expectation rather than of dread?

18. Having completed a study of Isaiah, if you were asked to briefly describe the central message of the prophet Isaiah, what would you say?

ABBREVIATIONS

Books of the Bible

Gen—Genesis
Exod—Exodus
Lev—Leviticus
Num—Numbers
Deut—Deuteronomy
Josh—Joshua
Judg—Judges
Ruth—Ruth
1 Sam—1 Samuel
2 Sam—2 Samuel
1 Kgs—1 Kings
2 Kgs—2 Kings
1 Chr—1 Chronicles
2 Chr—2 Chronicles
Ezra—Ezra
Neh—Nehemiah
Tob—Tobit
Jdt—Judith
Esth—Esther
1 Macc—1 Maccabees
2 Macc—2 Maccabees
Job—Job
Ps(s)—Psalm(s)
Prov—Proverbs
Eccl—Ecclesiastes
Song—Song of Songs
Wis—Wisdom
Sir—Sirach
Isa—Isaiah
Jer—Jeremiah
Lam—Lamentations
Bar—Baruch
Ezek—Ezekiel
Dan—Daniel
Hos—Hosea
Joel—Joel
Amos—Amos

Obad—Obadiah
Jonah—Jonah
Mic—Micah
Nah—Nahum
Hab—Habakkuk
Zeph—Zephaniah
Hag—Haggai
Zech—Zechariah
Mal—Malachi
Matt—Matthew
Mark—Mark
Luke—Luke
John—John
Acts—Acts
Rom—Romans
1 Cor—1 Corinthians
2 Cor—2 Corinthians
Gal—Galatians
Eph—Ephesians
Phil—Philippians
Col—Colossians
1 Thess—1 Thessalonians
2 Thess—2 Thessalonians
1 Tim—1 Timothy
2 Tim—2 Timothy
Titus—Titus
Phlm—Philemon
Heb—Hebrews
Jas—James
1 Pet—1 Peter
2 Pet—2 Peter
1 John—1 John
2 John—2 John
3 John—3 John
Jude—Jude
Rev—Revelation

NOTES